THE DWELLING PLACE OF DEITY

II Peter 2: 5 "Ye also, as lively stones, are built up a spiritual house, an holy priesthood, to offer up spiritual sacrifices, acceptable to God by Jesus Christ"

Dr. Wayne Hinson

All scripture quotations are from the
Authorized King James Version
All songs referenced are in the public domain
Copyright © 2022 Dr. Wayne Hinson
All rights reserved under the U.S. Copyright law.
Published by Dr. Wayne Hinson

Printed in the United States of America

**U.S. Copyright No. 1-11160172021
ISBN: 979-8-9857408-0-6**

DEDICATION

After 74 years on this earth and after 47 of those years as a God-called preacher of the gospel of Jesus Christ, I could not begin to comprise a list of all those men and women who have influenced my life. That list would be longer than the pages of this book. Only heaven will offer the time and opportunity for me to thank each one of them. But there is that one special person who always elevates to the top of the list. That special person is my wife, Mary. Although she is afflicted with severe back problems, she still rises above the pain to help me with proofreading and to add thoughts of her own as I write. She is a constant source of encouragement and enlightenment to this preacher. Above all that she does and all that she means to me, I have to say that the constant reminder that she loves me, is the fuel that keeps my life running.

…Doc

TABLE OF CONTENTS

INTRODUCTION 7

CHAPTER ONE: The Listing, A House for Sale 15
I. Price Must Be Determined 17
A) pre-qualification to purchase 18
B) prior mortgage 21

II. Property Must Be Described 22
A) the size of a soul 22
B) the scene in a soul 23
C) the supremacy of a soul 23

III. Profit Must Be Detailed 24
A) a finished transaction 26
B) a firm title 27
C) a proven truth 28
D) a promise and a token 28

CHAPTER TWO: The Lodging, A Home for The Spirit 33
I. Moving in day 34
A) Conversion of the house 34
   1. the room of reception 34
   2. the room of repentance 35
   3. the room of redemption 36
B) Cleansing of the house 38
   1. a funeral service is held 39
   2. a family celebration is held 40
C) Control of the house 40

II. Maintenance on Duty 42
A) The Caretaker 43
   1. he empties the trash 44
   2. he unpacks the truth 44
   3. he turns on the utilities (water, lights, heating/AC) 46
B) The Custodian 50

CHAPTER THREE: The Living, A Haven for The Saint 53
I. The Housewarming Event – The Furnishings 54
A) the living room 55
B) the study room 56
C) the career room 57

II. The Heartwarming Event – The Food 60
A). A New Diet 61
    1. milk 61
    2. bread 62
    3. meat 63
    4. fruit 64
B) A New Direction 67

CLOSING 69

CONTACTS 70

INTRODUCTION

When the subject of Deity is presented in conversation, most of us automatically think of God in heaven. Others may become a tad bit more Biblical and think of Jesus' earthly ministry. Still others that are a bit more dedicated, will allow their thoughts to travel to Calvary and see Jesus hanging on the cross. We have no problem visualizing God dwelling in heaven or acknowledging that Jesus dwelt here on this earth for 33 ½ years. Likewise, we are prone to recognize God's presence in nature and we are quick to boast of God's presence in the blessings that we receive.

All these thoughts that recognize God's dwelling places are excellent thoughts, and thoughts that should not just be passing thoughts. Theologically, all that I have mentioned so far are the foundational beliefs of Christianity. But, there is much more that these facts that magnify the dwelling place of deity. In God's dwelling place always at a remote setting? Do we not keep Him at a distance so as to feel more comfortable? Have we not tuned our spiritual engines to only operate with God at a reasonable distance?

To attempt to answer these questions and more, let us travel back to the Old Testament administration of the Holy Ghost. Sad to say, most Christians are not aware of the fact that the Holy Ghost deals and administers differently in different times or administrations. In the

Old Testament, the Holy Ghost never indwelt a single believer. He would come upon a believer and empower that believer to do service for the Lord. When that particular service was completed, then the presence of the Holy Ghost for that specific task, would leave that person. As it was in some cases, the Holy Ghost would stay with a person for long periods of time, such as was the case with Moses. This explains why David pleaded with God in Psalm 51:11 *"take not thy Holy Spirit from me."* If the administration of the Holy Ghost was the same in the Old Testament as it is in the New Testament, then David's plea would mean that a saved person could be lost again. We know that is not true, so we must recognize the truth that there have been different administrations.

The men and women that were chosen by God for service in the Old Testament, performed great and mighty acts and deeds for the Lord God, and they did it with only the presence of the Holy Ghost upon them, but never were they indwelt by the Holy Ghost. How much more should we that are indwelt by the Holy Ghost do for the Lord? This fact raises the question of why did the Holy Ghost deal differently with people in the Old Testament than He does now. The answer is two fold. One part of the answer is Calvary and the other part is the day of Pentecost. Old Testament saints looked forward to the promise of Calvary by faith. Calvary then serves as the dividing line between the two different administrations.

You will recall that when Jesus was preparing to ascend back to heaven, He told His disciples that He would send them another comforter. He also instructed them as to where to gather and that they should dwell in that place until the answer came. That very second when the Holy Ghost filled the upper room, the Old Testament administration of the Holy Ghost came to an end and a new and more glorious administration began. Never again would He empower a believer from without, but would always henceforth empower believers from within.

One other thought needs to be discussed at this point. You will recall that David wrote in the 23rd Psalm these words *"I will dwell in the house of the Lord forever."* He also stated in Psalm 27:4 *"One thing have I desired of the Lord, that will I seek after; that I may dwell in the house of the Lord all the days of my life."* David could not correctly say what Peter penned down in our chosen text because David lived under a different administration of the Holy Ghost. David's statement was referring to his being a member of God's family and therefore a member of God's house. David was speaking of dwelling with God, but Peter is speaking of God dwelling in him. In verse 4 of chapter 2, Peter refers to the building as a *spiritual house*. In this present administration, when a person is born again, the same Holy Ghost that convicted them of their sins, now takes up His residence in the soul of that newborn child of God.

Let's go a little deeper into the well of God's Word. When God created Adam, He created him in His image. That does not mean that man looks like God but does mean that God created Adam as a triune being. A triune being is one that can manifest themselves in three distinct and different personalities. We know that God is one God, but also can manifest Himself as God the Father, God the Son and God the Holy Ghost. One God but three distinct and separate personalities of communication. When He created Adam in His likeness, Adam was one man who could manifest himself in the realm of communication in three distinct and different ways. Mankind can communicate with their minds, with their bodies and with their spirit or soul. The mind and body is of a temporary nature since Adam and Eve sinned in the garden. Their sin separated them from a relationship with God. Because of that, the body and mind will die, but the soul of man is eternal. The body and mind of man is now not capable of communicating with God. Deity only comprehends deity. But the soul of man is eternal and after the Holy Ghost quickens that soul that is dead in trespasses and sins, that soul is made alive unto God. The Holy Ghost then takes up His residence within that soul and hence, deity can communicate with deity.

Jesus said, *"I am come to seek and save that which is lost."* Who is Jesus talking about? He is referring to every created human being that has ever been born on the face of this earth. That means that Jesus came to this earth with only one purpose and that purpose was to love and locate humans with lost souls.

In essence, Jesus came to this world seeking property to purchase. Not only was He searching for lost property, but He was willing to pay the purchase price for that property before He ever gained control of that property. This price was one that man could not pay, but the God-Man could pay. Jesus died on the cross of Calvary, shed His precious blood, was buried, but arose on the third day. He had defeated death, hell and the grave. 40 days later, just before His ascension back to heaven, He declared *"I will send you another comforter."* What purpose was that Comforter to carry out? Please do not miss this. His sole purpose in this present administration to occupy all properties whose present owner would sign the deed over to Jesus Christ. Do I really mean that God the Holy Ghost will open the door to your house and make it a home? By all means, the Holy Ghost will confront a lost soul, convict a lost soul and convert a lost soul. At the exact second of conversion, the Holy Ghost opens the door to your property and moves in.

I hope that I have successfully brought you through the Word of God and that I have succeeded in enlightening you as to how the Holy Ghost operates in our present day of grace. I hope that you now understand that Jesus has bought and paid for every piece of soul real estate and that He sent the Holy Ghost to seek out, save and secure those properties. My question to you: Have you opened the door to your house and allowed the Holy

Ghost to move in?

It is a sad thing indeed that most Christians have a "past tense" thought pattern which only includes their salvation experience. They maintain that there was a time when the Holy Ghost came calling and knocked on the door of their soul. They affirm that they responded to that knock and opened the door. However, there has been no progression in their life since that day. This amounts to nothing more than a "past tense" Christian life. They are adamant when they say that the ticket has been bought, but they have done nothing more that occupy a seat at the airport where they are waiting for their flight out.

We also have those that maintain they are going to heaven. Yes, they will talk briefly about their salvation experience, but the main thrust of their conversation is about heaven. These are the "future tense" Christians. Strange as it may seem, they are always talking about heaven and all their family and friends that they will reunite with, but their conversation never includes Jesus Christ. Their thinking has spilled over into the church society and the world system to the degree that everyone is going to heaven these days. To this crowd, Jesus is always "future tense."

Now, it is very true that if you are redeemed by the blood, you will have a testimony of that day when God saved your soul. It is also true that if you are born again, you will have a longing for heaven. These are foundational truths that every believer will have. The point that I am trying to make is that while you should have a "past tense" Jesus and you should have a "future tense" Jesus, is there not a whole spiritual universe that you are missing if those two tenses of Jesus is all you have in your life?

Perhaps you have already guessed where I am headed. There is a tense of Jesus that most Christians today have forgotten about. That tense is the "present tense" Jesus who is the owner of the property of your soul. He is not just the "past tense" Jesus who saved your soul and He is not just the "future tense" Jesus who awaits your arrival in heaven. He is that "present tense" Jesus who walks with you every minute of every day. Jesus is that friend who will never run off. Jesus is that fortress that will never fall down. Jesus is that fact that will never fade away. Jesus is that fellowship that will never forsake. That blessed old hymn that still rings loudly in my soul says it better than I can.

He lives, He lives, Christ Jesus lives today
He walks with me and talks with me
Along life's narrow way

He lives, He lives, salvation to impart
You ask how I know He lives,
He lives within my heart!

CHAPTER ONE
THE LISTING – A HOUSE FOR SALE

We have already established the truth that the primary mission of our Lord Jesus Christ's ministry on this earth is to seek, save and secure spiritual real estate. This real estate property is the souls of all mankind. II Peter 3:9 *"The Lord is not slack concerning His promise, as some men count slackness, but is longsuffering to us-ward, not willing that any should perish, but that all should come to repentance."*
I realize that some of you are already wondering about the title of my first chapter *"A house for sale,"* but if you will stay with me, I believe I can justify that title with Biblical truth.

Your soul, which is your spiritual real estate property, is for sale. Not only was the primary mission of our Lord to seek and secure spiritual real estate, but it is also the primary mission of Satan. Not long after God created Adam and Eve, Satan appeared on the scene and placed his bid for the souls of both of them. Of course, Satan was not willing nor able to pay for their souls, but was waiting to get their soul property by default. Their acceptance of Satan's lies caused them to sin and their sin separated them from God. As a result, God cast them out of the garden. Their sin cast them into a state of a lost condition. Hence, every descendant of Adam and Eve are also in that lost condition. In our world today, a property can become condemned for one reason or another. Until the reason that property was condemned has been taken care of, then the property is of no value. Make note that Adam and Eve were in a perfect paradise garden because we will discuss the parallel between that garden and the garden that the Holy Ghost wants to build in every soul property that will come to Him in repentance.

Except for Satan's evil deed in the garden, he really does not have to do anything to gain ownership of a lost soul property. Along with that truth, you need to know that you do not have to do anything either, because that property is already condemned and lost without God. That soul according to Ephesians chapter 2, is dark, dead and barren already. Satan is playing a waiting game because he knows that unless a person is born again and relinquishes the title deed of that property to Jesus Christ, then he will obtain ownership by default, and that soul property will wind up in hell. In other words, a person who does nothing to change the lost state of their soul property, that soul property will wind up with Satan in hell.

I. A PRICE MUST BE DETERMINED
I Peter 1: 18-20

"Forasmuch as ye know that ye were not redeemed with corruptible things, as silver and gold, from your vain conversation received by tradition from your fathers; but with the precious blood of Christ, as of a lamb without blemish and without spot"

When a property is listed in real estate, a market price has to be determined. This is usually achieved by having an appraisal done. The appraiser establishes the square footage of the house, the number of rooms in the house, the value of other properties nearby and location, location, location. All these findings are factored together and what is called "a fair market price" is determined. In the case of your soul property, the redemption price is far above all that mankind possesses. The price is far above all the money in all the banks in all the world. If the world system could gather all the money on earth, all the real estate on the earth, all the possessions on the earth, and assess the value of it all, the price for your soul property would far exceed that amount. Not only is there a problem with anyone having the quantity of the price of your soul, but there is also:

A) Pre-qualification to purchase

"Forasmuch as ye know that ye were not redeemed with corruptible things, as silver and gold, from your vain conversation, received by tradition from your fathers"

In today's real estate market, a proposed buyer must qualify themselves in advance or their offer will not be accepted. In other words, they must establish that they either have the cash money or they have been approved for a loan from a financial institution. Now, let us apply all this information and facts to the spiritual property called a soul.

Peter lays the facts on the table in verse 18 as quoted above. This verse is addressed to those who are already redeemed. By reading between the lines of this statement, we can accurately determine that corruptible things such as silver and gold, vain conversations and traditions are not qualified to purchase the real estate property of a soul. Silver and gold represent the riches of this world. Vain conversations represent religion and all other ways devised by man to get to heaven. Tradition takes care of all the sects, cults and fables that have been handed down through the years. All are dis-qualified by the Word of God. In God's Word, we find it said that the *"wages of sin is death"* and therefore we can determine that someone has to die as payment for our sins. Not only did the purchaser of the soul property have to die, but God's only acceptable payment is the blood. All through the Old Testament, the blood line that produce a Saviour was protected and preserved by God Himself. For His chosen people of Israel, God instituted and allowed the sacrificial system of the blood of an animal to be presented to God by the High Priest in the holy of hollies. Year after year, sacrifice after sacrifice, blood after blood, the sins of the people were covered by these sacrifices. They were covered but those sins piled up year after year. But then came that Friday afternoon in history, when the darling Son of God, the incarnate God-Man called Jesus Christ, climbed up on a cross called Calvary and made that one time for all time sacrifice of His death and the shedding of His innocent blood. That one sacrifice did not cover any sin, but that one time sacrifice washed away the penalty of sin, which was death. No more dead animal sacrifices, no more entering by the High Priest into the holy of hollies. That system was now dead forever. The Bible declares that the veil that separated the people from the holy of hollies and that veil that God allowed only the High Priest to enter into, was torn from top to bottom. Every believer, as a result of that action, no longer needs a go between priest, but now has access into the very presence of God.

By this act and this act alone, Jesus Christ pre-qualified Himself as not only the redemption purchaser but also the redemption price of the real estate property of your soul. No one else could meet the requirements or the standards. No mortal man could ever pay the asking price because the one that had to die must be sinless and no human ever meets that qualification. The price that was paid for you real estate property is now being held in an escrow account and it remains your decision as to whether or not you will accept what God has done and whether you will transfer the title deed to that property to God. John 3:16 *"For God so loved the world, that He gave His only begotten Son, that whosoever believeth in Him, should not perish but have everlasting life."*

In chapter 1 and verse 20, Peter adds a golden nugget to this wonderful state of Jesus Christ being qualified. *"who verily was foreordained before the foundation of the world, but was manifest in these last times for you."* Did you catch that nugget? While this tremendous truth is too vast for my finite mind to grasp, I am going to try and explain what part of it that I do understand. Since God is God, He has all foreknowledge of all things and all eternity. That simply means that God has the ability to see everything that will occur before it actually physically occurs. In the wisdom of His foreknowledge, God saw that Adam and Eve would fall into sin in the garden. Because of His power, God could have destroyed them on the spot, or worse still, He could not have created them in the first place. But over and above His foreknowledge and His power was His love for mankind. Before the first 911 call about the first sin of the first sinner, God had foreordained His Son, Jesus Christ, to be the sacrificial Saviour for sinful man, and God provided His Son as the first responder bringing salvation. That Friday afternoon in history, was the physical acting out of a predetermined decision. Salvation was a done deal before God ever created Adam and salvation was a public deal that day at Calvary.

B) Prior mortgage

At the actual closing of a sale of real estate property, evidence must be presented that verifies that there are no liens or active prior mortgages against that property. This is not an option since the law requires that a "title search" be conducted by a qualified attorney. This investigation must show evidence that the property in question has what is called "a clean and clear title."

If we would conduct a title search on the property of a soul, then it would reveal that a mortgage was placed against that property when Adam and Eve sinned in the garden. The actions of those two plunged all succeeding mankind into a state of sin and a state of being lost without God. Satan, who orchestrated this event, is now in line to receive the property, not by payment, but by default. That includes every person on planet earth, past present and future. Satan is now in line to receive the property of all souls by default, which means that he never paid a dime for them.

II. THE PROPERTY MUST BE DESCRIBED

During my 47 years of studying the Word of God and having read hundreds of books written on various Bible subjects, I have never read any material that even remotely attempts to describe the size or dimensions of the soul. After much meditation and prayer, I have decided that I will tackle that subject. May the good Lord guide my heart as I address the subject of:

A) The size of a soul

Scripture does not inform us of the size of a soul, but there are some facts stated in scripture that would give us an indication of its size, when taken into consideration and weighed in the balances. For example, a soul must be of great dimensions because God the Holy Ghost takes up His residence and dwells in the soul of a believer. Not only does He dwell there, but since there is only one God who manifest Himself in three distinct personalities, we must conclude that all three persons of the Godhead are also present in the soul of a believer. Another fact to be considered is the omnipresence of God. God is large enough to be in all places at all times, but as massive as that fact seems, He is still housed in the soul of every believer. Our same God is also present in the past, present and future of eternity. I would conclude that our soul must be of a vast dimension.

B) The scene in a soul

Ephesians 2:1 tells us that our soul was *"dead in trespasses and sins."* It also informs us that the Holy Ghost quickens or makes alive our dead soul. To me, that means that the soul of an unbeliever is dark and barren. Since that dead soul has no life, then it also has no light and no heat. It is a cold and dark place. This describes a barren property. Until and if there is a quickening of the property of your soul, there is no means of communication with other human beings or with God Himself. Dead is dead.

C) The supremacy of the soul

This subject goes all the way back to the creation of Adam in Genesis 2:7 *"and the Lord God formed man of the dust of the ground, and breathed into his nostrils the breath of life; and man became a living soul."* The supremacy of the soul has nothing to do with the soul's ability to act, either negatively or positively. It has everything to do with the fact that God breath His breath into Adam and Adam became a living soul. That act is further described by the fact that God created Adam in His own likeness. That likeness is not how Adam looked but that his soul was eternal. The soul of mankind will exist forever, either as a born again child of God or as a hell bound child of the devil.

III. THE PROFIT MUST BE DETAILED

I Peter 1: 4-5 "To an inheritance incorruptible and undefiled, and that fadeth not away, reserved in heaven for you. Who are kept by the power of God through faith unto salvation ready to be revealed in the last time"

Peter vividly sets forth a picture of our inheritance and makes plain the fact that it is reserved in heaven, and it does not fade away. What is this inheritance? It is everything that God has in eternal riches. Jesus said in John 14:2 *"in my father's house are many mansions; if it were not so I would have told you. I go to prepare a place for you"* This promise tells us that there is profit in relinquishing the title deed to our soul property to Jesus Christ in salvation. Brethren, that is giving up our claim to our real estate property and in exchange, we will receive our own real estate in heaven. That's right, we are now property owners of real estate in glory land.

The words that Peter declares *"to an inheritance incorruptible and undefiled"* are close kin to Ephesians 1:13 *"ye were sealed with that Holy Spirit of promise, which is the earnest of our inheritance until the redemption of the purchased possession, unto the praise of his glory."*

Both passages indicate that we have an inheritance in heaven and that inheritance is sealed, incorruptible, promised, undefiled and that the presence of the Holy Ghost in our souls, is the earnest of our inheritance.

The Greek word for *"sealed"* was used extensively in the commercial industry of that day. It refers to the sealing of a building. This act was to guarantee a piece of property against theft. It was also used as a marking seal on such things as a sack of grain. The seal was place on the sack until the full payment was made. In this word's many definitions, we find that it means to make a mark denoting ownership. It is also a mark that speaks of approval or closure of something. It also is defined as a certification that something is true. Its' further definition includes that a seal was used to serve as a guarantee of correctness of the contents. From these wonderful definitions we further note that the indwelling of the Holy Ghost is a guarantee that no one or no power can steal that soul. To further protect this property, the Holy Ghost, upon entering the soul, shuts the door behind Him and places the seal of God as a measure of security and ownership. That means that this soul property now belongs to God and it also means that this soul property can never again be without the ownership of God. The presence of the Holy Ghost in a soul further announces that God has moved into the premises and that the premises have to be cleaned and that nothing that defiles can now enter the property. The presence of the Holy Ghost also indicates that He is there as a resident until the day of redemption. That day of redemption will be the rapture of the church, the taking away of the saints of God, both alive and dead. That will be the day of the glorification of the body, which was not eradicated in salvation.

A) A finished transaction

These two sections of scripture are also kin to John 19:30 where Jesus uses the Greek word *"tetelestai"* which literally means *"paid in full,"* just before He died on the cross. The history of that word which means *"paid in full"* is when a Roman citizen was convicted of a crime, the law of that day locked him in a prison, and a certificate of debt that listed all his crimes was prepared and nailed to the door of his cell for all the world to see. It would remain there to guarantee that he served his full sentence and that the penalty for his crimes was "paid in full." The three words "it is finished" which our Lord uttered from the cross, are actually one word in the Greek language, and that one word means *"paid in full."* Spiritually speaking, we were guilty of crimes against God. We were in sin's prison with no possible way of release. A certificate of debt had been prepared listing all our crimes against God. That document was nailed to the door of our prison, which is our soul, and there we remain without hope. That is, until that day in history, on a Friday afternoon, just before the last breath left the body of our Lord Jesus, He exclaimed these words, *"it is finished"* which means *"paid in full."* Oh bless the day when the Holy Ghost pulled up his chariot of grace at the door to my soul. Oh bless the day when I heard of what Jesus had done for me. Oh bless the day when I realized through conviction and conversion that my sin debt was gone. Oh bless the day when I learned that Jesus had paid in full all of my sin debt.

Oh, bless the day when I heard that God remembered my sins no more and that they had been buried in the depths of the sea. Now instead of that certificate of debt hanging on the door of my soul, there is a new certificate of deliverance hanging there. And when the devil visits me and tells me that I am not saved, I just show him that certificate of proof that my sins have been forgiven and that my debt has been paid in full.

B) A firm title

In Biblical days, the buyers of timber would walk the forest and would select the trees that they wanted cut and place a stamp of their personal seal on that tree. The tree would be cut and carried to the sea where it would be floated down stream to the port of Ephesus and there it would be claimed by the owner, who could identify the chosen tree by the seal he had placed on it. Our soul, likewise, has been stamped with the seal of promise, which is the Holy Ghost, and our soul has been cut loose from the world and has been harvested from the world. We are not being floated downstream, but we are being floated upstream to glory land, where we will be identified by the seal placed on our soul and claimed as God's property.

C) A proven truth

A seal was used in ancient times as proof of authenticity or of identity. Everyone had a unique seal that they used for identifications purposes. Those with seals would become known by their seal. When passing a piece of property, passersby would converse with one another and confirm the ownership of that property by the name of the owner of the seal.

Illustration: when I was a child, I often visited my grandparents who lived on a farm. As was customary in those days, all of their neighbors were farmers as well. What intrigued me was the term that my grandparents and neighbors used to identify a particular farm or piece of property. They would say, for example, "that is the John Smith home place." As this memory came to mind, I could not help but apply it to the indwelling of the Holy Ghost in my real estate property. We could very well and with accuracy, refer to our soul property as "home place of the Holy Ghost."

D) A promise and a token

The Holy Ghost, as the caretaker and manager of the soul real estate property, is actually paying us interest on our inheritance. Ephesians 1: 13-14 informs us that this interest is the *"earnest of our inheritance."* The word *"earnest"* means *"pledge."* It was made as a promise that full payment was forthcoming, When an earnest was given, it guaranteed that the final pay was secured and would be made. The joys, delights, gifts, leadership, peace, love and grace are all earnest payments or interest on our inheritance. Our present blessings and benefits are just tokens of the great inheritance that is reserved in heaven for us.

Illustration: In our country, we use paper money to transact our daily affairs. To coin the phrase, "it is not worth the paper it is printed on," the paper money we use certainly fits that description. However, it is backed by pure gold that is held in reserve at Fort Knox KY. In a like sense, the benefits we now receive and enjoy as a child of God, would not worth any permanent value if they were not backed by our inheritance in the bank of heaven. We are just receiving installments from our inheritance. The caretaker of the property is making daily deposits into our account.

Our inheritance is also our heritage. It is not given to us simply because we deserve it, and we may not lay claim to it according to our own merits. It is ours because we are loved by God with an infinite love that gave Jesus Christ up and placed Him on Calvary where He died in our place. It is ours because we have been born again into the family of God as sons. I John 3:2 *"beloved, now are we the sons of God."* As Peter states plainly, it is *"incorruptible"* which means that the gnawing teeth of decay cannot corrupt it. Moth and rust cannot consume it. Thieves cannot gain control of it. No spend thrift can claim it.

It is *"undefiled."* There are not any stains from the world system on it's pure robes. Not a dark spot on the leaves of its' fruit trees. Not a trace if this life's storms in it's atmosphere. Everything negative in this world is stopped at its' gate.

"That fadeth not away." Its' brightness will never be dimmed; its' beauty will never be tainted' its' bond will never be broken; its' boundary will never be breached; its' building will never be broken into; its' blessing will never be blocked; its' builder will never be bankrupt; its' blossom will never be withered; its' benefits will never be depleted. Its' basket will never be emptied; its' banner will never be defeated; and its' birthright will never be stolen.

"Who are kept by the power of God." The concept used here is that the children of God are being brought through enemy territory with an armed escort. Their protection is in direct accordance with the level of power that escorts them. We are not in glory land yet, but when we consider the power of the armed guard that is supplied to us, which is the Holy Ghost, we are as safe now as if we were already home. How much power does our armed escort have? He was able to create this universe and all that is contained within. He is able to control this universe by placing His finger on this earth and causing it to spin in rotation from the sun, which gives us our nights and our days. He was able

to connect and communicate with mankind by sending His Son to be incarnated into flesh and become the God-Man. He is able to convert the vilest of sinners by His amazing grace. He is able to cancel the sin debt of every lost sinner. He is able to come back just as He did the first time.

There is even more profit to be gained in this real estate transaction. John penned these wonderful words in I John 3:2 *"beloved, now are we the Sons of God, and it doth not yet appear what we shall be, but we know that when He shall appear, we shall be like Him."* Not only are we the Sons of God now, but John declares that when Jesus shall appear, we are going to look like Him. I do not know about you, and I do not know what Jesus looks like, but when He comes back for the saints, I am going to look like him. That means that not only do I have the family inheritance, but I am going to have the family likeness. You see, my soul has had a blood transfusion. All the blood of evil and sin has been removed, and the blood that was shed on Calvary for my soul's redemption has been injected into my soul. That family likeness comes from the blood. I have been bought with a price and the blood of my soul is now the blood that paid that price. I will be like my elder brother, the Lord Jesus Christ.

CHAPTER TWO
THE LODGING – A HOME FOR THE SPIRIT

In the Old Testament administration of the Holy Ghost, God dealt with believers through a promise, but in the New Testament administration of the Holy Ghost, God deals with believers through a possession. A believer must possess the Holy Ghost in order to possess Christ. Let me add a note before we move ahead. The property of your soul is dead according to Ephesians 2:1. You do not have the power nor the privilege to change the condition of your soul property. With that said, every person does have the right and the option of refusing the purchase price that has been paid. Once again, you have that choice. But you need to know that refusal of Christ's finished payment for sin and the purchase price of your soul property, will send your soul to hell. Notice that I said that what you do and what you decide will send your soul to hell. That is exactly correct. God has done all that He can do to keep your soul from going to hell and now it is in your hands. Have you made the right decision?

Since the soul of man is dead, that means that your soul could not seek God. It is dead and dead things do not move, speak or travel. The wonderful truth is that God came seeking for your soul. By virtue of that great truth, let us look at:

I. MOVING IN DAY

I Peter 2:5 *"Ye also, as lively stones, are built up a spiritual house"*

Before the door of your soul property can be opened, there are three divine transactions that must occur. Without all three transactions enacted and settled, the Holy Ghost will not grant salvation to the sinner. They are:

A) CONVERSION OF THE HOUSE

This conversion of the house of the soul takes place in three distinct rooms. They are:

1. The room of reception

The Bible declares that *"faith cometh by hearing and hearing by the Word of God."* In chapter 1 verse 25, Peter declares *"but the Word of God endureth forever, And this is the Word which by the gospel is preached unto you."* Therefore, the truth remains that a lost soul must hear the Word of God and must act by faith on what he has heard. Once again, Peter declared that *"the gospel is preached unto you."* The gospel by definition is the death, burial and resurrection of Jesus Christ. A lost person's faith must accept, believe and act upon the gospel which is preached unto them. When confronted and convicted by the preached Word of God and the presence and power of the Holy Ghost, the lost soul must receive the truth of what they have heard. God appropriates the gospel to the lost soul at His choosing. The lost soul must apprehend the gospel through the convicting power administered by the Holy Ghost and must accept that same gospel through faith. The Holy Ghost comes knocking on the door of your soul and you must open that door to Him. Once inside the door, you must invite the Holy Ghost to sit down in the reception room. You must welcome Him into your soul. Not only the room of reception, but we also see:

2. The room of repentance

Chapter 2 verse 4 *"who His own self bore our sins in His own body on the tree."* The second transaction that must occur on moving in day will take place in the room of your soul called the *"repentance room."* In this room, you and the Holy Ghost must have a face to face encounter. He will show you and convict you of the sinful state that you are in and will show you what Jesus did for you on the Cross of Calvary. That news will convict you soul that you are hopelessly lost without the intervention of Almighty God. You must repent. Repentance, by definition, is to do an *about face* in your life. It also means to do an *abrupt forsaking.* In country boy vernacular, you cannot take the offer that has been presented for the property of your soul, unless you make the turning from your sinful condition and forsake all sin in your life. The only part of this transaction for the lost sinner is a simple "take it or leave it."

I personally believe that every sinner will be offered the truth through the preaching of the Word of God. John 3:16 *"For God so loved the world, that He gave His only begotten Son, that whosoever believeth in Him, should not perish but have everlasting life."* Salvation is not a done deal until the sinner is done dealing. However, there is never a mention or the smallest indication recorded in God's Word, that says that God is obligated to send the gospel to a lost sinner more than once. God may, but then God may not. We have discussed the room of reception and the room of repentance, but there is a third room that must be visited on the moving in day of the Holy Ghost. That room is:

3. The room of redemption

I Peter 1: 18 *"forasmuch as ye know that ye were not redeemed with corruptible things, as silver and gold, from your vain conversation, received by tradition from your fathers."* Again, in verse 23 *"being born again, not of corruptible seed, but of incorruptible, by the Word of God, which liveth and abideth forever."*

Unfortunately, we live in those days when God's requirements for purchasing the real estate property of a soul, has been weakened by many false prophets, both in the pew and in the pulpit. In the world's religion, everyone goes to heaven. Just attend some funerals or listen to what is said when a celebrity or sports figure dies. However, according to God's infallible Word, these beliefs are nothing more than Satan's smoke screens to keep lost sinners from hearing the truth. Sad to say, and the proof is in the pudding, that many Christians are accepting this lie of the devil. In churches all over this country, when the occasion of prayer requests arises, the bulk of those requests will be for the infirmities of the flesh. Since everyone is going to heaven, there remains no need for the requesting of prayer for the lost.

In God's Word, this truth still remains, *"I am the way, the truth and the life. No man cometh unto the Father, except by me."* Peter added these words about false doctrines when he stated *"from your vain conversation."* The word *"vain"* means *"empty, without any possibility of proof, futile, ignorant and blasphemous."*

Now, if we apply that definition to the other word Peter uses, which is *"conversation,"* we will see that this description is an exact match for the false doctrines of today.

Let me declare that God is still in the redemption business. In my most recent visit to the throne room in prayer, I saw no sign that said "closed" or "going out of business." Redemption is the bringing out of a sinner from their lostness, while being born again adds that sinner to the family of God. That old song from yesteryear still rings in my soul. It goes like this:

Blessed Assurance, Jesus is Mine
Oh, what a foretaste of glory divine
Heir of salvation, purchase of God
Born of His Spirit, washed in His blood

This is my story, this is my Song
Praising my Saviour all the day long

My dear reader, is this what you have in your soul? Have you been whitewashed by false prophets or have you been washed white by the blood of the Lamb? Redemption is the acceptance, the application and the action upon of the gospel of the Lord Jesus Christ. Nothing more and nothing less.

B) CLEANSING OF THE HOUSE

There is a term that is used in the house cleaning industry that fits perfectly here as a description of what has to occur when the Holy Ghost enters the real estate property of your soul. He does not enter without a purpose. That term is "deep cleaning." It involves a thorough cleaning of every inch of a house. I believe that this is what II Corinthians 5:17 actually is referring to when it declares *"old things are passed away, behold all things are become new."* Your soul, in it's lost state, was dark, dirty because it housed all your sins and your sinful nature. But now, your soul has been redeemed and your soul has been born again into the family of God. A new and glorious day has dawned in the property of your soul. The Holy Ghost has just moved in and nothing will ever be the same. The events that take place during this house cleaning are:

1. A funeral service is held

II Corinthians 5:17 *"old things are past away."* That term *"past away"* is still used today in reference to someone who has died. We will say that they have past away. In our society, when someone passes away, a funeral service is held. That relates very well to what occurs in your soul when this house cleaning takes place. The Holy Ghost will begin to decorate your house with all new furnishings. The old furniture that you used before, has to be done away with. The Holy Ghost will not take that furniture to the 2nd hand store, where someone else could purchase and possess it. That old furniture is headed for the dump. Your old spiritual clothes which resemble grave clothes have to burnt or buried because they will not fit you new soul. The Holy Ghost will supply you with a brand new wardrobe of grace clothes that will be tailored made to fit. Your property no longer has any connections to former things and former sins. The Holy Ghost is performing a thorough house cleaning, and is going to present you with a spiritual housewarming. We will discuss that house warming and the gifts a little later in our study. The furniture, clothes and decorations that were there for your past life will no longer suffice because you are now in God's family. At the funeral of things that have past away, the Holy Ghost might say "let the dead bury the dead."

2. A family celebration is held

When the house is cleansed, there has to be a celebration that is twofold. There will be a housewarming shower given and there also will be a baby shower given. The reason for the housewarming is that there is everything is now new and the Holy Ghost has brought gifts to give to the new soul. But also, Peter gives validity to the baby shower when he writes: *"as newborn babes, desire the sincere milk of the Word."* He also says in 1:14 *"as obedient children, not fashioning yourselves according to the former lusts in your ignorance."* Your soul has a new family, new brothers and sisters, a new elder brother and a new father. In this celebration, you will be bottle fed from the Word of God. The Holy Ghost will begin to teach you all the wonderful things concerning Jesus Christ.

C) CONTROL OF THE HOUSE

In salvation, the soul is redeemed and born again in the family of God, but the flesh which is the old man or nature, remains the same. The old nature is not eradicated during the salvation of the soul. The truth that applies here is that the control of your soul has been turned over to its' new owner, but the body which is the old nature still belongs to you. There are two different houses and there are two different owners. No part of your body, your old man, your old nature can enter into the house of your soul. The Holy Ghost has shut the door and sealed the door to the soul property. But the reverse of that truth can happen. You can submit your body as a living sacrifice which Romans 12:1 plainly states. *(note: see my book on Romans 12:1-3 "Guided Steps To A Godly Sacrifice").*

When the redemption of your soul occurred, there was still a vast darkness there. But when the Holy Ghost moves in, He turns of the light. Jesus said, "I am the light of the world," and that is the light that the Holy Ghost turns on. Not only was there no light in your soul property, but there was no heat. Your soul was a cold dark and baron place. The Holy Ghost builds a fire in your soul that can warm your life for service to God. This what I have often referred to a "Holy Ghost Fire." That fire is eternal and will be burning nice and bright twenty four hours a day. When you are chilled by the trials you may be facing, just take a trip to the living room of your soul and sit down by the fire. When you have turned cold by some life experience, just come and sit around the fire and chat with the Holy Ghost. When you feel like quitting, just walk that path to the fire room in your soul and let the Holy Ghost tell you all about your Saviour. This world is a cold place for the child of God. People, including God's people, can inflict pain in your life. Family can leave you helpless at times. But in those times, just trot on down to the family room of your soul where a warm fire is always blazing.

II. MAINTENANCE ON DUTY

Before I begin to develop the subject of the maintenance that the Holy Ghost performs upon entering your soul, I feel the need to challenge and correct, by scripture, an erroneous and even devilish doctrines that are prevalent today.
When the New Testament was completed, which occurred during the first century after Christ ascended back to heaven, special revelation such as was given to the Apostle Paul ended. We now have the complete Word of God. We do not need and should reject any new additions or so-called revelations.

The first doctrine that I am challenging is that which says that God gives special rank and revelation to certain men. Roman Catholics think that special revelation from God is given to the pope. According to their doctrine, these revelations take precedence over the Word of God. Naturally this results in contradictions and confusion. They maintain that Mary remained a virgin all of her life, and was without sin. They further believe that they have direct access to God by praying through the virgin Mary. Their further belief is that the presiding Pope stands in the place of Christ and directly receives revelation from

God. This doctrine and this cult remains prevalent in today's religious world. This is a prime example of how man's religion can directly contradict the Holy Ghost. Additionally, a born again child of God can never be a part of a one world church.

When the Holy Ghost takes up His residence in the property of a soul, He performs maintenance in accordance with the Word of God. God is no respecter of persons. They are no elite its in God's family. One believer does not have any special access to information or revelation that another believer does not have. In the process of performing maintenance on the property, the Holy Ghost assumes the role of:

A) THE CARETAKER

The dictionary defines the word "caretaker" as "one who cares for buildings and grounds of specific properties and lives on the premises to provide better surveillance and security." Now that is enough to make the quietest of church members shout. I will use that definition to further magnify the role of the Holy Ghost as the caretaker of the property of your soul that was bought and paid for by the blood of Jesus Christ. The duties of a caretaker are:

1. He empties the trash

The unsaved property of the soul is in a state of sin. Since it is subject to the desires and sins of the flesh and also of Satan, there are mountains of trashy sins that life has dumped on the property. The garbage of evil desires and ungodly deeds are piled everywhere. This would be an overwhelming task for anyone else, but the Holy Ghost can handle it in a hurry. The first duty of the Holy Ghost as caretaker is to empty all that trash that has accumulated during your unsaved life. Peter acknowledged this action when he wrote in chapter 2 verse 1 *"wherefore laying aside all malice, and all guile, and hypocrisies and envies and all evil speakings."* The strength and power of the old nature is still active and that old nature wants to remain on the throne, but the Holy Ghost as caretaker, is stronger and more powerful and will empty your soul of all the old trash that has accumulated.

2. He unpacks the truth

In the words of our Lord in John 14:26 *"but the comforter, which is the Holy Spirit, whom the Father will send in my name, He shall teach you all things, and bring all things to your remembrance, whatsoever I have said unto you."*

You will notice that all three persons of the godhead and the trinity of God are mentioned in an active part of this verse. Jesus alluded to the fact that the Holy

Ghost, as a caretaker of the soul, is to be a teacher of the truth that Jesus spoke. Jesus further documented this fact in John 15:26 when he said *"But when the comforter is come, whom I will send unto you from the Father, even the Spirit of Truth, which proceedeth from the Father, He shall testify of me."* Once again, please note that all three persons of the godhead were mentioned in this verse in an active capacity. In further documents the fact that the Holy Ghost as a caretaker will unpack the truth of the Word of God in your soul is found in John 16: 13-14 *"Howbeit, when He, the Spirit of truth, is come, He will guide you into all truth, for He shall not speak of Himself, but whatsoever He shall hear, that shall He speak, and He will shew you things to come."*

Let's take the last seven words that Jesus spoke in verse 14 *"He will shew you things to come."* Now we know that Jesus brought truth to this world while in His earthly ministry. Jesus is the incarnate Word of God. What we have to understand is that the truth that Jesus brought to this world, has to be unpacked, taught and explained. Only deity can accomplish that feat. Only deity can comprehend deity. Therefore, the role of the Holy Ghost as the teacher of all the truth concerning Christ, has been established. However, Jesus plainly declared that the Holy Ghost would not magnify Himself but would magnify Jesus Christ. Since Jesus is the Word that was in the beginning and the Word that was made flesh and dwelt among us, that means that the curriculum at the school house in your soul will be nothing else but the infallible, inerrant Word of God.

3. He turns on the utilities

The utilities of a home are generally considered to be water, power and some source of heat/air conditioning. The Holy Ghost will take care of turning on the spiritual utilities on your property. All three sources of spiritual utilities can be substantiated in the Bible. I Corinthians 2:14 states *"but the natural man receiveth not the things of the Spirit of God, for they are foolishness unto him; neither can he know them because they are spiritually discerned."* The things of God that are not seen by the human eye are the utilities that He turns on when He indwells the property of your soul. Notice with me as I address all three utilities. They are:

WATER

Ephesians 5:26 states *"that He might sanctify and cleanse it with washing of water by the Word."* The Holy Ghost uses the medium of the Word of God as His foundation for all that He will teach. When He turns on the water source on the property, He is turning on the fresh supply of the revealed Word of God. The faucet in your soul will always bring forth an ample supply of God's Word.

Illustration: When I think of a water source on a piece of property, I have to recall the well that sit on the hill on my grandpa's farm. They never had running or piped in water. On that well house, there was a well-worn aluminum bucket, which was attached to a well-worn rope that was wrapped around a cut log that had been mounted on the well house. There was a handle on that cut log. In order to get water, you would have to drop the bucket into the well and just after you heard it hit bottom and splash, you would begin to turn the handle and draw the bucket up. When it was drawn up, there was always a dipper hanging on a nail and you could dip yourself the best drink of water ever.

I said all that to say this. The Holy Ghost is a well of living water that abides in your soul. Just as Jesus told that Samaritan woman in John 4 *"but the water that I shall give him shall be in him a well of water springing up into everlasting life."*
That well that sat on the hill on my grandpa's farm was a source of life to them. When they wanted water to drink or for cooking, regardless of the weather and regardless of what time it was, they had to go to the well for water. Hallelujah, that is what we must do. There is water in the well and that well is in your soul and the Holy Ghost will allow you to come and draw up a dipper full of that living water.

LIGHTS

When the subject of utilities comes up in conversation, the mention of power or lights will be near to the top of the list. When God created this world, one of the first things He did was to turn on the light. Genesis states that right after God created this earth, that it was dark and void. The reason for this condition of the earth was that there was no light source. So God said, *"let there be light."* Now notice that it was the spoken Word of God that produce light. That is all that Almighty God had to do. We can take that truth and apply it to the indwelling of the Holy Ghost. Your soul was dark and barren, but the Holy Ghost opened the door and spoke the Word of God and there was light. The presence of deity always brings light. When Jesus was born and the angels announced His birth to the shepherds, the Bible declares that the *"glory of the Lord shone round about them."* That glory was the light of God. Then Jesus declared that "I am the light of the world." The Apostle Paul, while traveling on the Damascus Road, was blinded by the light of Jesus Christ.

In Psalm 119:105 *"thy Word is a lamp unto my feet and a light unto my path."* In Psalms 97:11 *"Light is shone for the righteous."* In Psalm 119:130 *"the entrance of thy words giveth light."* In accordance with the Word of God and the spoken command of Jesus, which came through the Father, the Holy Ghost is going to turn on the light of the will and word of God. No more darkness in your soul property. That light will light up your spiritual walk with God.

Illustration: When I was a young boy and made a wrong decision about something, my daddy would always correct me. In that correction, he would always say, "let me shine a little light on that, son." This is how the Holy Ghost guides you in your daily walk with Jesus. He will shed a little light on your decision making.

HEATING AND COOLING

We had discussed in detail the turning on of the water and of the lights in your new house, now we turn to the subject of heating and cooling. Jeremiah said that when he was ready to quit on God, he would not speak any more in His name. But then the Word of God was in his heart as a burning fire shut up in his bones. John the Baptist preached, *"I indeed baptize you with water; one mightier than I is coming, whose sandal strap I am not worthy to loose, He will baptize you with Holy Ghost and fire."* And so, the Holy Ghost upon entry into your house, lights a fire that is eternal and shall never fail. This world we live in can be cold, but then at times it is like a hot burning desert. Regardless of how cold it gets or how hot it gets; the Holy Ghost has turned on the heat pump and the air conditioning and the welcome mat is out.

In summary, let me add a wonderful thought that was conveyed to me by my dear friend and brother in Christ, Dr. Arthur Moore of Vanceburg Kentucky. His words were: "the devil comes around from time to time and tells me that my bill is past due, and he is going to shut off my utilities. That is when I remind him that my bill is set up on auto pay from the bank of heaven and is paid in full by the blood of the Lamb. I think that says it better than I could even think it. Hallelujah.

B) THE CUSTODIAN

The dictionary defines the word *"custodian"* as *"one who is entrusted with guarding and keeping property. One that guards, protects and maintains property. Historically, it means one who has possession of all the keys to a property."* The Holy Ghost certainly qualifies as a custodian of the real estate property of the soul. That property has been bought and paid for by the blood of the Lord Jesus, and the Holy Ghost has moved in and now resides on the property. He does possess the keys to God's Word, as well as the gifts of the Spirit. His custodial work includes regular house cleaning which a believer must have in order to maintain a quality spiritual life. His main concern is the care and welfare of the child of God. He operates in the realm of a believer's soul and that environment has been purified by the washing white of the blood of the Lamb. His custodial concerns also involve the leading and guiding of the saint so as to live more wholesome, healthier and holier lives. The Holy Ghost cleans house and keeps that house clean.

Another aspect of the custodian of the soul is that He is a mentor to the believer. I Peter 1: 13-15 *"wherefore gird up the loins of your mind, be sober, and hope to the end for the grace that is to be brought unto you at the revelation of Jesus Christ. As obedient children, not fashioning yourselves according to the former lusts in your ignorance. But as He which hath called you is holy, so be ye holy in all manner of conversation."* We are called children in this passage, which alludes to our new birth into the family of God. As spiritual children, we are very susceptible to peer pressure. If we are not careful, we will be poured into the mold of the world system. For this and many other reasons we must obey the mentoring of the Holy Ghost. Peter uses the term *"former lusts."* Let me say that these lusts are still active in the old nature and if you give them an inch, they will quickly take a mile. Peter's exhortation in these 3 verses is aimed at our having daily sessions of instruction with our mentor. The mentor will teach a new believer how to control those old lusts and how not to be controlled by them.

CHAPTER THREE
THE LIVING – A HOME FOR THE SAINT

I Peter 2: 1-5 *"Wherefore laying aside all malice, and all guile, and hypocrisies, and envies, and all evil speakings. As newborn babes, desire the sincere milk of the Word, that ye may grow thereby. If so be ye have tasted that the Lord is gracious. To whom coming, as unto a living stone, disallowed indeed of men, but chosen of God, and precious. Ye also, as lively stones, are built up a spiritual house, an holy priesthood, to offer up spiritual sacrifices, acceptable to God by Jesus Christ."*

In the Old Testament administration of the Holy Ghost, God dealt with believers through a promise, but in the New Testament administration, God deals with believers through a possession. In the Old Testament, God dealt with believers from the outside inward, but in these days, God deals with believers from the inside outward. That possession is a property called the soul. That soul which is redeemed is the real you. The flesh is not the real you, unless you have never been redeemed. I have said all that in order to say this. If you are redeemed, the property of your soul, that Jesus has purchased and the Holy Ghost resides, is your new home. In Acts 17:28, these words add credence to this truth, *"For in Him, we live and move and have our being."* Also note the words of promise from Jesus in John 14:23 *"If a man love me, he will keep my words, and my Father will love him, and we will come unto him, and make our abode with him."* The Greek word for "abode" is the same word used for "home."

Now for you, the reader, to fully understand the descriptions that I am going to use, you will have to leave your thoughts of the physical realm behind and enter into the spiritual realm. There are areas of spiritual though that cannot be comprehended by the physical mind. Just remember that the spiritual person is now who really are. Notice with me:

I. The Housewarming Event – The Furnishings

In society, when a family purchases a new home, especially their first home, their friends and family will give them a housewarming shower. At this event, gifts that will aid that family in furnishing and decorating their new home, would be presented to them. Spiritually speaking, your new home, the soul, is no different. A *'housewarming shower'* has been planned by the Holy Ghost. He also has an abundance of spiritual gifts for you. The Holy Ghost is an expert in the art of decorating and furnishing new homes. Every gift He gives, will be perfectly suited for your home. What a thrilling and joyful occasion it is as you begin to unwrap each individual gift the He has brought and given to you. The list of these special gifts is: charity, joy, peace, patience, kindness, goodness, generosity, faithfulness, modesty, self-control and chastity. These gifts will completely and perfectly furnish the rooms of your new home. There is one more event that will occur in the living room of your new home. Peter declares in chapter 1 and verse 23 *"being born again."* Then he goes a step further in his declaration and states in chapter 2 and verse 2 *"as newborn babes."* It is a truth that just as a physical birth yields a newborn baby, the spiritual birth also yields a newborn baby. This housewarming and the presentation of the spiritual gifts is nothing more than a *"baby shower."* We all know that the gifts at a baby shower are directed toward the growth and development of the baby. All these baby shower gifts will be systematically used as the growth of the newborn baby develops. The very first room that will be furnished is:

A) THE LIVING ROOM

Ephesians 2:6 *"And hath raised us up together and made us to sit together in heavenly places in Christ Jesus"*

The living room of a home gets its' name from the fact that this is the room where most of the living in a home is done. This room can also be called a family room. It exists for the purpose of relaxing, meditation and fellowship. The living room of your soul, which is your spiritual home, is no different. Three of those spiritual gifts will be place in this room. They are love, joy and peace. This room will be decorated with mutual love between you and God. There will be pictures on the walls that are placed there to remind you of just how much Jesus loves you. The mutual love that fills the air in the living room now produces joy. This joy is not of the world's variety but is joy that originated in the joy world of heaven and has been shipped to your soul. This joy is so great and wonderful, that the Bible declares that it is unspeakable and full of glory. Because this living room is filled with love, joy and peace, you can sit here and enjoy the view. Ephesians 2:6 *"And hath raised us up together and made us sit together in heavenly places in Christ Jesus.* This verse tells me that even though we are in this world, we can, through the picture window provided by the Holy Ghost, catch a glimpse of our heavenly home. Once again, not physical but spiritual applies here.

B) THE STUDY AND CHAPEL ROOM

As I write this book, I am sitting in my study. This room is a special room with a special atmosphere and furnishings that are conducive to my meditation and writing, but also serves at times, as a chapel where I can worship God, pray to God and even have a shouting spell. It is like no other room in our house. It is unique and every item and piece of furniture in this study, serves the purpose of supporting my work, my writing and my worship. The same holds true with the spiritual study and chapel of your soul. It is "a get away from the world" room and one where you can be alone with God. The atmosphere and environment of this room in your soul home is like no other because it is where you can meet and meditate with God the Father, God the Son and God the Holy Ghost. And the only language spoken in this special room is that of the infallible, inherent Word of God. Yes, it is heaven on earth. This is the room where you can go when trials and temptations come your way. A place where you can have a little talk with Jesus and that will make it right.

C) THE CAREER ROOM

Most Christians and yes, most preachers never consider that being a child of God has also given them an eternal career. The dictionary defines the word *"career"* as *"a course, a race, a pilgrimage, a procedure and a walk."* I do believe that according to this description, we have a career with God. The career room in your spiritual home is a multi-functional room. Allow me to elaborate:

1. It is a classroom

John 14:26 *"but the Comforter, which is the Holy Ghost, whom my Father will send in my name, He shall teach you all things, and bring all things to your remembrance, whatsoever I have said unto you."* When God redeems your soul and adds you to the family of God, you were added as a newborn baby. Newborn babies do not know how to talk, walk or eat. They have no knowledge of how to take care of themselves or how to deal with the world system. Yes, they have to be taught and that instruction is conducted by the teacher and counselor, the Holy Ghost. In this classroom, you learn step by step the ins and outs of living for God. The only curriculum textbook that is used in this classroom is the Word of God. You will never graduate from this school, but you will gradually, step by step, achieve a closer and higher walk with God. You will never learn it all and you will never achieve perfection in this life. The truth is, that you cannot walk one spiritual step without the aid and assistance of the teaching of the Holy Ghost. The truth is that not only does He teach you how to take that first step as a newborn baby, but also becomes your helper by holding your hand, in every step you take in life. The truth is that a newborn baby has no sense of direction. Without the Holy Ghost as your guide, you will wander aimlessly in your spiritual life. Sad to say, this is the lifestyle of so many Christians today. They have wandered so far from God, that they have forgotten where they came from. Many of them have no clue where they are going in their spiritual life. You cannot work for God without guidance, and you will never know the will of God without a counselor. Your tuition is paid in full, and you cannot fail in this school unless you do not show up for class.

Another area of instruction that takes place in this career room is of family fellowship and relationship. Yes, you have been born into a brand-new family and you have new brothers and sisters, which includes your Elder Brother, the Lord Jesus Christ. You have a new father who is God. Your total relationship has changed and now the Holy Ghost will teach you how to fellowship with your family.

2. It is a counseling room

My wife Mary spent most of her life teaching school. She also served as a principal in three different schools. I have learned from her, in various conversations, that in many cases, she would have to counsel a student before that student could be taught. This is an area in the church world today that has been neglected. With the rise of false teachings by some television evangelists, people are led to believe that they can gain spiritual insight from the Word of God, regardless of how low their lifestyle is. But it doesn't work that way. One television evangelist teaches that you should surround yourself with people that agree with you and celebrate your life. By falsely stating that you should surround yourself with people that agree with you, is in essence, saying that you have no negative aspects nor any sin in your life. It just does not work that way. This is why the career room is also a counseling room. Your physical deformities will stand in the way of your spiritual affirmatives. In the course of serving as pastor for 35 years, there have been multiple occasions when I was asked to counsel people. I was, and still am, a little hesitant to do so, for fear that I am not qualified to perform that task. Looking into this counseling room, we will discover that the Holy Ghost is highly qualified since He is God and He counsels using the Word of God. If you want to be a success in your career for God, then knowing the will of God for your life is an absolute must. You are not going to find out what that will is, anywhere else except in this classroom and counseling room. The world system and its' technology does not know the answer. Even your brothers and sisters in the family do not know the answer. Only God knows this answer and His chosen way of revealing that answer is for you to sit in the classroom and sit under the instruction of the Holy Ghost.

II. THE HEARTWARMING EVENT – THE FOOD

When God created man, He did so with the plan that man would replenish his physical body with food. Whether we will admit it or not, consuming food is at the top of the list when it comes to the needs of the body. Adam and Eve, while in the garden of paradise, eat from the fruit trees that God supplied. It should not surprise us that a redeemed soul is born again with a spiritual appetite, and it should not amaze us that God has a supply of spiritual food that is perfectly suited for the soul's replenishing. These facts bring us to the most important aspect of the home which the Holy Ghost is now maintaining. Yes, that is correct, we are now in the kitchen of your new home. Notice with me that the newborn soul has an appetite for:

A) A NEW DIET

Please understand that before redemption, our physical bodies were addicted to wants, desires and appetites of the flesh. Since the soul was dead in trespasses and sins, there was no spiritual appetite, therefore there was no spiritual food. These appetites of the flesh still remain in the physical realm of the body. The Holy Ghost will prepare a new diet for the believer. It will contain spiritual foods from the garden of the Word of God. Your new diet consists primarily of milk, bread, meat and fruits. You will be fed from these food groups, but not all at once. You are a newborn baby, so the first item on your new diet will be:

1. Milk

I Peter 2:2 *"as newborn babes, desiring the sincere milk of the Word."* Do not be shocked when you discover that your entrance into the family of God was as a newborn baby. Babies cannot consume whole foods, so until they develop some, milk is their diet. They are bottle fed by the Holy Ghost. The milk of the Word of God will make them strong and healthy, that they might grow up to be strong and healthy spiritual adults. We need to discuss a subject that has and still is, a major problem among those who purport to be children of God. Their problem is that they have been saved by grace for twenty or thirty years and are still sucking on a bottle of milk. This lifestyle amounts to a gross contradiction of Biblical interpretation.

2. Bread

Jesus declared that "I am the bread of life." He did not come into this world to establish a homeless shelter which hands out free bread. He came into this world to be the bread of life. He did not come to satisfy your physical hunger for bread, or for any other fleshly desire or need. Jesus came to change your desires for earthly things. He became the bread of life so that you would taste of that heavenly bread and therefore your desire and appetite would also change. May I declare that there is fresh bread in the oven of the kitchen that the Holy Ghost oversees. He is a master chef and He serves up Jesus, the bread of life, at every meal. The oven in His kitchen is never turned off. Oh my, the aroma that drifts out of His kitchen is unreal. There is an open invitation from Him for you to come and taste of this heavenly bread. During the first phase of your childhood as a member of God's family, you will be fed from the milk bottle. This is all that your spiritual system can process. But the day has to come when the Holy Ghost will take away the milk bottle and begin to feed you the Bread of life. Your spiritual teeth have not yet developed, but you can eat bread, especially that heavenly bread that the Holy Ghost dips in the milk of the Word of God.

3. Meat

I have wondered for 74 years why certain back teeth are called *"wisdom teeth."* Now this is most likely Hinson-ology, but it makes good sense to me. First, a spiritual baby is fed milk simply because they are not developed enough to handle anything else. Then comes the bread dipped in the milk and then after a few front teeth show up, the Holy Ghost begins to feed them bread alone. Now, back to the *"wisdom teeth"* theory. *"Wisdom teeth"* are jaw teeth that are there for the purpose of chewing food such as meat. The Holy Ghost is aware that a newborn baby does not have any teeth, much less wisdom teeth. During the first two steps of feeding a young spiritual child, that child of God has gained wisdom from the sincere milk of the Word and the Bread of life which is Jesus. It takes spiritual wisdom to consume the meat of the Word of God. The Apostle Paul, while addressing the church at Corinth, stated that he would have given them mean but could not. They were not ready for meat. They were still being bottle fed with milk. They had not matured enough to have cut their *"wisdom teeth"* and therefore could not chew spiritual meat. Right after Paul discussed the "wisdom" of God in I Corinthians 2: 6-7, he immediately began to convey to the Corinthians that he wanted to feed them meat, but they were yet so carnal, he told them they were not able to digest meat. The presence of carnality always results in the lack of spiritual wisdom. In other words, they had not developed enough to have *"wisdom teeth"* and as a result, could not consume the meat of the Word of God.

Let me add this thought before I move on to the next item of your spiritual diet. *"God has no dumb children."* If you profess to be a child of God, then you are born into the family of God with a spiritual appetite for spiritual food. I repeat, *"God has no dumb children."* Maturity is a definite sign of having been born again. The lack of maturity in a professing child of God is a direct contradiction to everything that the Word of God teaches. So, if you are redeemed and washed in the blood, then proceed to the kitchen of your soul property and let the master chef, which is the Holy Ghost, feed you that heavenly diet.

4. Fruit

Galatians 5:22-23 *"But the fruit of the Spirit is love, joy, peace, longsuffering, gentleness, goodness, faith, meekness, temperance, against such there is no law."* I see three very important points in these verses that the Apostle Paul wrote to the church at Galatia. In their proper order, they are:

A. Vices

Just before penning down verses 22-23, Paul records an enormous list of vices that are common to the flesh. Notice, first of all, that these are listed plural, but when he records verses 22-23, the uses the singular version of fruit. Being plural means that the vice life is a matter of choice. The is a long list of vices or sins that the world system and the flesh have to offer. You can pick and choose from this list, but remember you are bound by your sin. In other words, you can pick your poison. Verses 19-21 shows us a list of vices and yes, you are a free moral agent, and you can choose between that list or you can choose all that list. The bottom line that Paul is drawing is that your choice between the two lists proves where you are in regard to salvation.

B. Virtues

As I have noted, the word "fruit" is singular. It is not recorded as "fruits." That means that in the kitchen of the Holy Ghost, you cannot pick and choose which virtue you please. It is a package deal and the list is administered by the Holy Ghost. Since they are a package diet, the order they are listed is not that important. This list of virtues is not laid out on the kitchen table by the Holy Ghost, with instruction to pick and choose your favorite. They are all one beautiful bouquet of flowers. Fruit is a beautiful bouquet of virtues.

Let us look at this in one more way. The word *"fruit"* is singular. There is only one fruit of the spirit, but that one fruit contain nine virtues. If one of the virtues is missing, then it cannot be the fruit of the Spirit. In mathematics, if a whole unit has nine parts and you remove one part, then that whole unit is not whole any longer. It becomes defective and so it is with the fruit of the Spirit.

One more view of this verse is that Paul added the words, "against such there is no law." Now we know that the law operates on perfection. In other words, if we break one point of the law, then we have broken all the law, but Paul declares that in essence, the law can find no flaw in the fruit of the Spirit, while there is an eternity of flaws in the vices of the flesh.

C. Venue

Every passage if scripture in the Bible, especially those in the New Testament, that details the work and will of the indwelling Holy Ghost, points to a garden being planted and cultivated in the soul property of a new believer. Remember, in previous discussions, that there is only one fruit tree, but that one tree produces nine different virtues that are to be fed to the child of God.

When the Holy Ghost takes up housekeeping in the property now owned by Jesus Christ, He plants a garden which He waters and cultivates. That garden will supply the fruit of the Spirit and that fruit will be served on the table in the kitchen room of your soul. The sincere milk, the bread of life, and the strong meat that have been amply fed to you, will always be available at the same table. These spiritual foods have served to grow you up into a mature child of God, and as you develop and progress from one stage of nutrition to another, and even though the necessity has changed, you can still supplement your diet with these foods.

We can easily see that milk, bread and meat are the appetizers, but now it is time for the main course, that is that wonderful life changing fruit of the Holy Ghost. Galatians 5: 22-23 "But the fruit of the Spirit is love, joy, peace, longsuffering, gentleness, goodness, faith, meekness and temperance." Just before Paul lists the virtues of the fruit of the Spirit, he details the vices of the flesh. We could say that the vices of the flesh are from the garbage dump of one's old nature. They look like garbage, and they smell like garbage, and they will produce garbage in your life. Then, after listing the vice of the garbage dump, he lists the virtues that can only come from the garden He has planted in your soul.

B) A NEW DIRECTION

When the Holy Ghost spreads the fruit of the Spirit on the table, the *appetite* of a child of God has to increase. A healthy spiritual appetite at the table in the kitchen of your soul property, will produce a healthy *attitude* when you get up and exit the kitchen. Healthy attitudes will produce healthy *actions* when you apply these virtues to your everyday life. When your spiritual actions are in line with the virtues that you have fed upon, then your heavenly *altitude* changes. Your appetite affects your attitude, your attitude affects your actions, and your actions affect your altitude. Now when you reach that altitude where you daily walk and talk according to the instructions supplied by these nine virtues, your *aptitude* will begin to increase at a steady and substantial pace. What happens then is that you find yourself back at the kitchen table with an even greater *appetite*.

CLOSING

It is my prayer that what I have penned down in this book, will broaden your spectrum of the indwelling Holy Ghost. It is my hope that something that was said in this book will enhance your performance as a child of God. It is my expectation that God's work on this earth has been advanced by something I have written in this book. I leave you with the one verse of scripture that has propelled and prompted me to write sermons for 47 years: *II Timothy 2:2 "And the things that thou hast heard of me among many witnesses, the same commit thou to faithful men, who shall be able to teach others also."*

In His Name....Doc

CONTACTS

For a complete list of publications, you can contact Dr. Hinson at:

7029 Hwy 81 North

Piedmont S.C. 29673

www.ingramcontent.com/pod-product-compliance
Lightning Source LLC
Chambersburg PA
CBHW060854050426
42453CB00008B/969